The Season

by Steve Bowman & Mark Stallings

A Photographic Look at the Sport of Duck Hunting

Foreword

The reason behind this book is a long time in coming. It actually started formulating itself in 1998, a few months after the Arkansas Duck Hunter's Almanac was published. That book's redeeming value was all the stories centered on the rich history of duck hunting in Arkansas.

This book is obviously much different; There are still many stories to tell, there always will be. Hopefully, what this book will do is show the reader what duck hunting really is through the images of a duck season in Arkansas, and through those images tell a visual story.

With the exception of a few choice images, the photos in this book were taken in the heat of the hunt during the 2005-2006 Arkansas duck season.

Steve Bowman and Mark Stallings spent the season traveling with hunters all over the state taking photos of every segment of the hunt. By the end of the season they, along with James Overstreet, had taken more than 7,000 photos.

All those images didn't make the book. But hopefully the ones that did, along with a few taken during previous seasons, will offer the reader, whether a duck hunter or not, a glimpse of what a duck season looks like through the eyes of a duck hunter.

Dedication

This book is dedicated to two of the finest men a duck hunter could ever share a blind with: Wendell Bennett (1961-2002), shown pointing to the sky, and Todd Carter (1963-2001), with a rainbow over his shoulder. Both of their lives were cut way too short. Todd's by cancer, Wendell's by drowning on a fishing trip. Their memory stays with us every day, as does their love for duck hunting. Ironically, these two photos were shot in almost the same exact spot in a rice field near Bald Knob, Ark.

Contents

Copyright © 2006 by Steve Bowman and Mark Stallings

Printed in the United States of America by Democrat Printing and Lithograph, Little Rock, Ark.

Layout and design by Michael Puckett, the Puckett Studio, Little Rock, Ark.

Cover design by Michael Puckett

Arkansas duck stamps provided by Larry Grisham, Grisham's Art, Jonesboro, Ark.

Pencil drawings provided by Larry Chandler, David Maass and Phillip Crowe

ISBN 0-9786952-0-8

Steve Bowman and Associates Publishing LLC
3115 N. Rodney Parham
Little Rock, Ark. 72212
501-221-2282

www.theduckseason.com

Acknowledgements

This book would not have been possible without the enormous help of so many people. It is a book our grandfathers would have described as a "picture book." It became a little more than that in the hands of Michael Puckett.

All we did was take the pictures. It was Puckett who made them come alive, turned them into photos and created the look and feel of this book. He deserves so much credit. His creative style is incredible.

All the creativity in the world, though, can't replace the support of family and friends, especially on a project like this.

A special thanks goes to:

Steve Bowman's wife, Barbara, and daughters, Melissa and Virginia (who appear in this book) have been invaluable. Bowman spends 30 weekends of the year away from home. Their support in utilizing what is left to complete this project is amazing. One might think they just wanted to get rid of him, if not for their occasional trip to get muddy and bloody in the duck woods with him.

Mark Stallings' wife, Dana, and sons, Evan and Carter, have provided unlimited support and encouragement. Dana kept the household running and continues to be more than just a wife but a best friend. Evan and Carter kept the farm running. Without their love, support and prayers, Stallings would not have had the inspiration or motivation to work through this project.

Others include: Steve Wright, who co-authored the Arkansas Duck Hunter's Almanac. His insistence this project would be worth the effort got us off our duffs.

Biff Morgan and Larry Grisham fall under that category as well. Grisham went a little further by enlisting friends like Larry Chandler, David Mass and Phillip Crowe, incredible artists, to provide the pencil drawings within.

James Overstreet, a longtime hunting buddy, who has become an incredible photographer. He's the expert who keeps us honest. A few of his images are featured in the book, simply because they are so good. Overstreet, we owe you.

Dave Greene, who became a tour guide; Jerry and Mike McKinnis, who let Bowman keep his job; along with numerous other friends and family who provided support and encouragement. Also, special thanks to everyone who allowed us to tag along and document their hunts.

And most importantly, we want to thank God for creating a world that includes ducks, men and women who love that creation, and the opportunity for us to show it to the rest of the world.

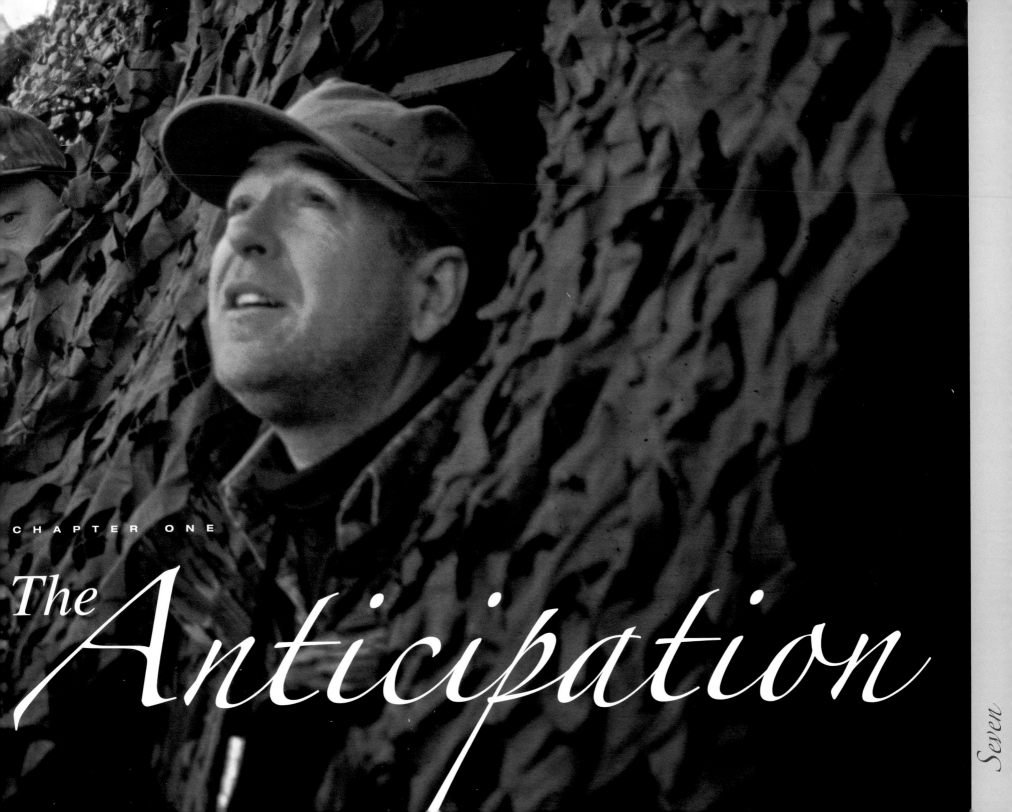

CHAPTER ONE

The Anticipation

an·tic·i·pa·tion
the feeling of looking forward, usually excitedly or eagerly, to something that is going to happen

That definition pretty much sums up a duck hunter's life. Everything he does in one way or another revolves around looking forward to a day of duck hunting.

It never really goes away, either. Around October it starts to gain steam. That's when the thrill of the chase and all those other nonsensical phrases begin to seep into a hunter's brain as they search for ways to explain their giddiness.

As an old duck-hunting friend is fond of reminding, "Everything I do is designed to waste time until duck season gets here."

Veteran duck season widows are well aware of the fact. That summer cruise, all those Mother's Day gifts, the help with drying the dishes, and compliments that start showing up about September 15 all become equity when the north wind starts blowing chilly air south.

A duck hunter can't help it; that anticipatory gene is just part of the DNA. He's almost driven by it.

Some of it might seem downright silly.

For instance, a duck hunter's anticipation is directly tied to the love life of a mallard. They don't think of it in those exact terms, but that's the case when a duck hunter anticipates the runoff from snow melting to the north in the late spring, filling breeding ponds, anticipating a great hatch of new ducks.

It carries over into late summer when news starts filtering out from biologists on just how many ducks will be available to make the migration. Then the anticipation kicks into high gear.

Weather reports are monitored like an ICU patient. Even the slightest bit of precipitation or change in temperature anywhere close to any of the right places and a duck hunter starts thinking about all the good things it might create.

The same guy who wouldn't mow the lawn a month earlier is pounding boards together for a makeshift blind, ripping up brush to hide it and reveling in the mud while thinking about all those wings that will be cupped over his decoys in a few weeks.

Then the season starts and hope springs eternal.

The weatherman is discussed, cussed and even occasionally applauded with forecasts that either add to or detract from the potential of the days ahead. But no matter how bad, it never, ever wipes out the thought that the right course of events is coming. It's during these times when the next cold front, regardless of its harshness, is looked upon with a childlike anticipation reminiscent of the days when Saint Nick was expected later that night.

When it gets here and it's so cold it chills down to the bone, duck hunters anticipate the sunrise of the next day. They look forward to the clanging of an alarm clock, the trip into the darkness to sit in the cold and wait. And when the sun washes light across the sky, anticipation is measured in increasingly smaller increments.

They anticipate the next hour, when surely the next wave of migrants will be enticed by the perfect cadence of hail calls and feeding chuckles. Then it comes to minutes waiting for the clock to finally tick to 30 minutes before sunrise, and the game is on.

It's present in the thoughts of when to make the next call, when to raise the gun, seeing the next retrieve or waiting for the last duck to fill the bag.

Anticipation never stops.

For the hard-core duck hunter, the anticipation of opening day is always there, even on the last day of the season.

Fourteen

It's All About The

Sunrise

It's been a decades-old lament.

A long, cold day spent hugging a pin oak or leaning against the muddy metal of a pit blind that ends with few ducks to show for the effort is justified by these words: "The sunrise was awesome."

You hear similar phrases a lot, even more so these past few years.

There have been so many days when there was too little water, too much heat and precious few ducks. It's the bane of existence for the modern-day duck hunter.

But one thing stays consistent: Every day starts and revolves around the sunrise.

It's the one thing a hunter can count on. And most days, when the sun starts peeking above the landscape, it is the most brilliant part of the day.

It can come in a fiery ball or, tempered with clouds, produce hues any rainbow would be proud of.

Twenty

Driving down the interstate, the sunrise is just light, forcing you to slide on your sunglasses to keep from plowing into the back of the next commuter. Sitting in a duck blind with the quiet of a day not yet awake, it's a completely different experience.

God's hand, like an artist brushing a canvas, is evident and awe-inspiring. The day has yet to take shape and everything is possible at that moment.

The scene has given rise to the phrase among duck hunters that the day sometimes boils down to being all about the sunrise.

The "all-about-the-sunrise" statement has been used so much that some duck hunters whisper it in disdain; others joke about it, while others sit quietly and appreciate it.

Twenty Two

Twenty Three

The sunrise is, after all, nature's alarm clock. It signals to the not-so modern ducks of the world that they've made it through the night. And for yet another day, it's time to get down to the business of making a living in the marshes, bottoms and fields of the world.

That makes it the most important part of the duck hunter's day. With the first rays of light, the game is on, at least somewhere. For every duck hunter who watches the world wake up, those first hints of light signal the first wave of hope that the ducks are playing in their part of the world.

The reality is the duck call means nothing. The gun can't be raised. The shot won't be taken or the retrieve made until the sun says it's OK.

When it comes to duck hunting, there is one never-changing constant ... it really is all about the sunrise.

Twenty Seven

Twenty Eight

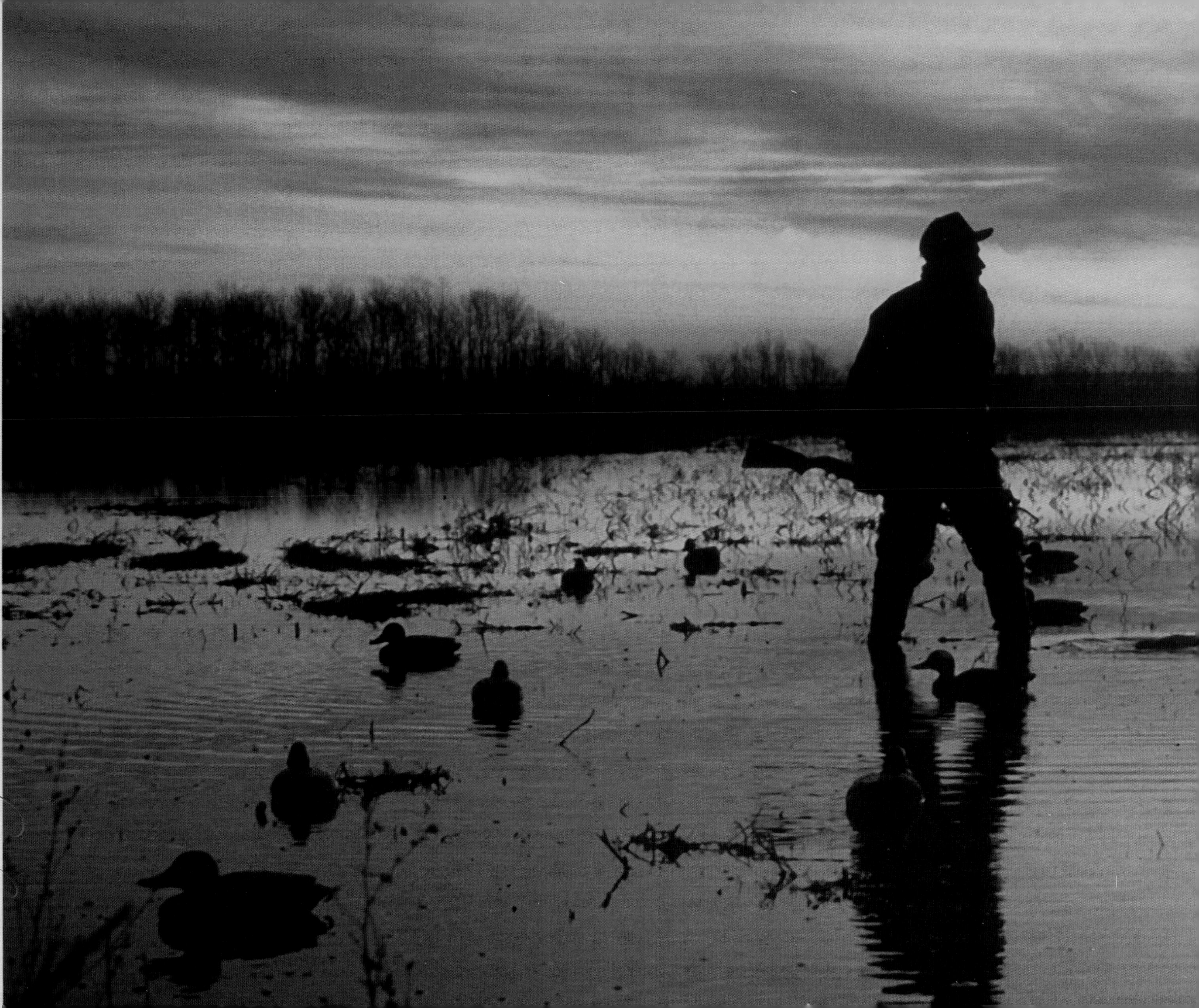

CHAPTER THREE

The Hunters

I t's a simple enough question: "What defines a proper duck hunter?"

It takes a lot to earn that designation. We're not talking about gentlemen hunts accepted in some circles. They involve hoity-toity places where dinner is served promptly at 7 and the undersides of your boots never leave a print in anything but the Zoysia path leading to a blind large enough to house a family and warm enough to hatch a nest of chicks.

Proper duck hunting is a little grittier, with mud and crud that seeps into every nook and cranny of things that don't even have a nook or a cranny. This is hunting with a pump or auto-loader, not because the proper hunter wouldn't love to shoulder an over-and-under, but because the other holds three shells and there are simply times when going to the plug with every round possible is necessary.

Thirty Three

That's the mantra of a proper duck hunter; he goes to the plug in everything, by throwing his heart and soul into every aspect of the hunt.

He spends weeks thinking about new ways to rig decoys; he can build more with a bunch of ratty camo and PVC pipe than MacGyver could ever dream, but he still hasn't completely figured out how to fix a thigh-high hole in waders for a hunt in crotch-deep water.

It's just part of the makeup of the proper duck hunter.

Along with other things, like boat motors that won't start, dogs that won't retrieve, guns that jam, partners who insist on calling even though they can't, days that are too hot, too cold, too dry, too wet or too almost everything else. The list doesn't stop: There's sky busters, call-shy ducks, hole-shy ducks, global warming, late-night card games, steel shot, cold coffee, hole sitters and bad shooters.

In the past decade, the proper duck hunter has seen duck numbers return to a level once only dreamed about, but the results in the day-to-day hunt have not borne that out. The proper duck hunter, in the pursuit of his sport, knows enough biology to make him dangerous. But he understands the perils of today's waterfowl, from habitat loss in Canada to

the degradation of hardwood bottoms to the south. He knows how a cold front can change his world, besides just making it cold. He can whisper barometric pressure and jet stream in the same sentence and is permanently addicted to the Weather Channel.

The proper duck hunter understands the nutritional value of acorns, rice, grass seed and even invertebrates and can recite their importance in the middle of munching on blind snacks that might provide sustenance but are far from healthy.

The proper duck hunter actually starts looking forward to the times when either he or one of his hunting party "floats his hat." That's a memory one must experience to become a member of the fraternity.

The average duck hunter would rather live with those impromptu baths than without them. Some of them actually need it, whether they like it or not.

It doesn't sound like something to look forward to. But without these things it wouldn't really be duck season to the proper hunter.

The proper duck hunter lives by the words of Robert Ruark, who summed up the feelings of hunters by simply writing "You've got to hurt to be happy."

In his "Old Man and The Boy" series of books he put it perfectly: "You ain't happy unless you're hurtin', and that somewhere in the hurt you cleanse yourself of a lot of civilized nonsense that spreads a thick veneer on the hides of people, like a scabby over-paint when what you really need first is a scrape job or a blow-torch. You scrape it off, you sweat it off, and you walk it off. Your head gets clearer, your senses sharper, and when you do come back—blistered, thirsty, too tired to be hungry, too weary to wash—some of the nonsense of today has been burnt away. Some beauty has been observed, some hardships overcome, some sympathies established, and there is a wondrous satisfaction about honest fatigue."

No truer words have ever been written. That's why the excitement of the hunt is not dampened by the fact that proper duck hunting can be downright painful. A pain that lasts for days, weeks, months .... and if a duck hunter's fortunate, years.

That is what the proper duck hunter looks forward to, and he wears it like a badge of honor. He knows the ducks, his ducks, are worthy of a certain sacrifice. He likes it better that way, and he feels something much more satisfying and deserving when he feels he's paid his dues.

To the proper duck hunter there are no such things as too cold, too hot, too early, too late, too far or too few.

They learn to live with the twigs and branches that got in the way of what they thought was a well-placed shot; alarms that didn't work; four-wheel drive vehicles stuck in the mud; idiots who shoot ducks on the swing; friends who claim every duck that hits the water; the nimrod your buddy invited who drops a

double-banded greenhead on the first shot; and yet another hole that shows up about thigh-high in your waders while standing in crotch-deep water.

By the end of the season, the proper duck hunter stands in the middle of his decoys, knowing he is picking them up for the very last time that season. He looks one last time across the landscape through raw, bloodshot eyes, and he hurts even more because he knows it's over.

From the outside looking in, it might not sound very appealing. But to the proper duck hunter, the one who understands that you've got to hurt to be happy, this is all bliss and a little bit more.

This is the definition of a proper duck hunter.

CHAPTER FOUR

The Next

Generation

As any parent will attest, children will often humble you.

It comes with the territory. Parents are supposed to pass things along to their children to teach them and to guide them. It's amazing how often those roles are reversed.

It happens a lot during duck season.

Duck hunters are fond of tradition. Passing along the ways of the duck hunt and all it encompasses to the next generation is something taken seriously in the flyways of America.

In a sport where conservation of habitat and the resource is the golden thread that binds, toting a youngster to a blind for a morning hunt is an obligation that fathers and grandfathers have met for generations. The next generation is charged with carrying on once we're all gone. At least that's the reason we give ourselves.

The reality is the relay of the tradition of duck hunting often comes in reverse when a child is on the hunt.

These stories are evidence. They revolve around the actions of the next generation and their feelings toward duck hunting.

On Virginia Ekenseair's first hunt in 1997, the 7-year old had tears in her eyes when she arrived at the duck blind.

It was the second time in several days that the emotion had shown up in regard to the hunt. Melissa Bowman, her stepsister, had cried, too. It was the afternoon before Christmas Eve when she planned to leave for the scheduled, traditional Youth Waterfowl hunt.

Fifty One

Fifty Four

The streets were icy and covered with sleet, and forecasts called for more of the same. There was no way her dad was taking a chance of not getting her home for Christmas. They could hunt another day. The other parents scheduled to go on the same hunt felt the same way. Melissa didn't. Her feeling was, if vehicles were driving down her street, they could go anywhere.

"If we go, then we might not get back for Christmas morning," she was warned.

"I don't care," Melissa said, sticking out her bottom lip and forcing big crocodile tears to her eyes. A combination of things she did so well for an 8-year old. She's a downright professional at it these days.

"I want to go duck hunting," was the emphatic response.

Despite the swell that can create in a father's chest, and a history of like-minded fathers succumbing to big tears and a bigger bottom lip, the decision stood. But at the first chance there would be a duck hunt.

When that chance came it was Virginia's turn to shed tears. She was packed on the back of a four-wheeler riding through a rice field. Water was flying, gumbo was churning and the motor was whining. For a 7-year old, it must have been a little imposing and a whole lot scary. All she could see was a sea of water in front of her that looked to be hundreds of feet deep instead of 4 inches. She thought they were headed to a watery doom.

But Virginia recovered right along with Melissa. In a blind surrounded by a blanket of fog, with hundreds of ducks and geese waking up just out of sight, teary eyes turned to wide-eyed excitement. Listening to sassy mallard hens quacking like they are in your back pocket with a chorus of whistling widgeons, laughing/half-quacking teal and the cacophony of snow and speckle-belly geese mixed in has a way of clearing the air.

In times like those, duck hunters learn the value of the next generation. It reminds us of the full gamut of emotions most of us have grown hard to. We forget how different it is to be sitting in a hole in the ground called a pit and surrounded by a sea of water, listening to sounds of birds that don't show up in your back yard.

We try at every opportunity to understand that. Even when so many ducks are in the air it's hard not to get excited right along with them.

Over the years we learn to stay grounded by taking those moments to survey the young hunters.

We wish we could regain the feeling that 5-year-old Jacob Carter had on the same hunt when there were hundreds of ducks sailing and circling above the blind. It was a mixture of everything the Mississippi Flyway has to offer, the ducks broken into small flocks of four to 10 and going in every direction. It can be an awesome sight, but when you're hunting and have that many different flocks sailing about, it can get downright maddening.

Jacob, though, reminded the veterans it didn't really matter. As each flock sailed over the pit, he would giggle, point his finger and shoot it with the same sound effects every kid makes when they play cowboys and Indians.

Jacob didn't know it, but he boiled duck hunting down to the simplest, best terms. You don't have to make a big bang, just get them close enough to look at, and you're having a great time pointing your finger and saying "pow."

There were other times as well, like when 15-year-old John Ekenseair was so thrilled about downing his first duck and two more that followed they were hoarded like a cache of gold, to be looked upon but not touched by anyone but him.

In times like those, duck hunters can learn a lot thinking of all the memories that each of them are storing. We start to get a little peek into what makes it so exciting for them. Is it sleeping in the bunk beds? Waking up when it's still dark? Wearing camo? Putting on new chest waders? Feeling a log bump along the

bottom of the boat and hearing the roar of the prop as it cuts air (this little activity always brings out gasps of "Cool!")? Just doing something radically different than other kids their age?

You quickly learn that we, the young and the old, go for different reasons. But we go together and that is what these days are all about, although every day should be like that.

They will always remember some part of those duck hunts. There's something they are hanging on to that will resurface again when they in turn tote their youngsters to the duck blind, to remind them of all the things they learned over the years about duck hunting and its real value.

CHAPTER FIVE

The Quarry

They come every year with positive regularity. But you can't set your watch by them.

A duck works on its own time, moved by the whims of nature. Driven by a need to escape the cold and find new food in an age-old trek, they sometimes travel in groups so large they can block out an airport's radar.

Their paths are marked by a system of rivers, creeks and landmarks — the original interstate highway system — that helps guide their way. A duck's life — revolving around a search for acorns, corn, rice, beans, seeds, invertebrates, water and even love — is in constant motion. It includes breeding in the spring, making a living for the hard trek in summer, then the trip.

Along the way they come into contact with a throng of humans completely bound to the area they live in, but entirely in love with the trip as it passes by.

The hunters of that group build blinds, dig holes, flood fields, train dogs and spend countless dollars and hours to have everything right when the ducks are in the neighborhood. Like the ducks, their lives are almost in constant motion for the trip. They have fallen in love with these travelers.

Much about duck season revolves around the pomp and circumstance of wearing camo, rigging decoys and tuning a call. But the thing that binds all of that together is the sights and sounds that waterfowl make during their yearly trip.

It might be the sun bouncing off the feathers of a greenhead as it banks around a set of decoys, the cupping and setting of wings of a brace of mallards or the distant sound of a lonesome hen quacking. They all create within a duck hunter something that makes them love these birds in a way others can't understand. He might not fully understand it, either. He just know it's there.

Seventy Seven

It's there before the sun breaks the horizon and the only signs of their presence are the sounds of whistling wings. It kicks into high gear when the morning air starts filling with flights of ducks. The game is on.

Any hunter can sit and watch ducks flying, sailing or cupping and get a charge out of it. But a duck hunter holds a special bond with these birds — One they create by pursing their lips and cranking out a highball or a subtle quack that produces a response. It's not like whistling for the neighborhood pet. These are wild creatures that understand the noises you make, and if you are good, makes them want to communicate in return and to come closer.

That relationship is the thing that draws us to these birds. We talk with them, sing with them and love sharing the same muddy environment with them.

We're drawn to their aerial acrobatics. We marvel at the unison of so many wings in perfect harmony.

We try to fathom how a flight of teal can instantly know to turn left, then right and do it again in perfect synchronization, or how a mallard can zig, zag and fight its way down through treetops with ease and lightly touch down with a grace man could never know.

They make us love them.

The thing that ensures that love will never die: They'll be back with the same positive regularity next year, doing it all over again and again.

CHAPTER SIX

The Retriever

Duck season would not be duck season without a retriever.

Sure, some folks hunt every day without one, but it is like a bad marriage. At some point in time you realize that something is missing. It comes hammering home when you enjoy the day with a hunter and retriever whose relationship is exceptional.

At that point it's hard to not want the same thing.

Retrievers have a way of fulfilling a duck hunter's life in ways that are hard to describe.

With apologies to author Gene Hill, whose prose could describe man's best friend like no other, these words are paraphrased by a fickle memory and certainly edited to fit the needs of a hunter in love with his retriever.

Eighty Nine

Every retriever owner feels the same way. It only takes a few days in the field to realize that a retriever is the best set of eyes on the hunt, with a gaze that can see through clouds and ears that can hear despite a strong north wind. He has senses that I can't fathom, and he's only too willing to share them whenever I need.

He is an extra set of legs that work for me in the flooded bottom or eight levees away in a rice field, with haunches that never tire and beg for more. I know that he will not stop until I need or want him to. But when I want him to, it's because I'm tired, not him.

He reminds me that everything I do is the most important thing in the world to him, especially if it means he can just be close to me, or better yet go and pick something up and bring it back for me.

His love for me is undying and constant, regardless of whether I have a half-eaten sausage and biscuit in my hand or an empty palm ready to scratch behind an ear.

He's never complained that I've showed up too early or too late, but when I do, the shaking of his tail starts at the tip and permeates all through his body just because I am there.

And when he sees me leave at an all-too-early time, dressed in camo and without him, the pleading in his eyes is so deep you would swear he'd never get over it. Yet, the second I return, covered with the scent of another, he's all too willing to forgive. He's just happy to know I survived, even without him.

There are no days too distasteful, too cold, or too hot when his time isn't best spent at heel and watching the clouds or listening to the wind.

He never chastises when I miss a shot, embellish a tale or hit the wrong note on a duck call. He lives for the moment when everything lines up perfectly and I bring those feathery retrieves from the sky to the water.

Ninety Seven

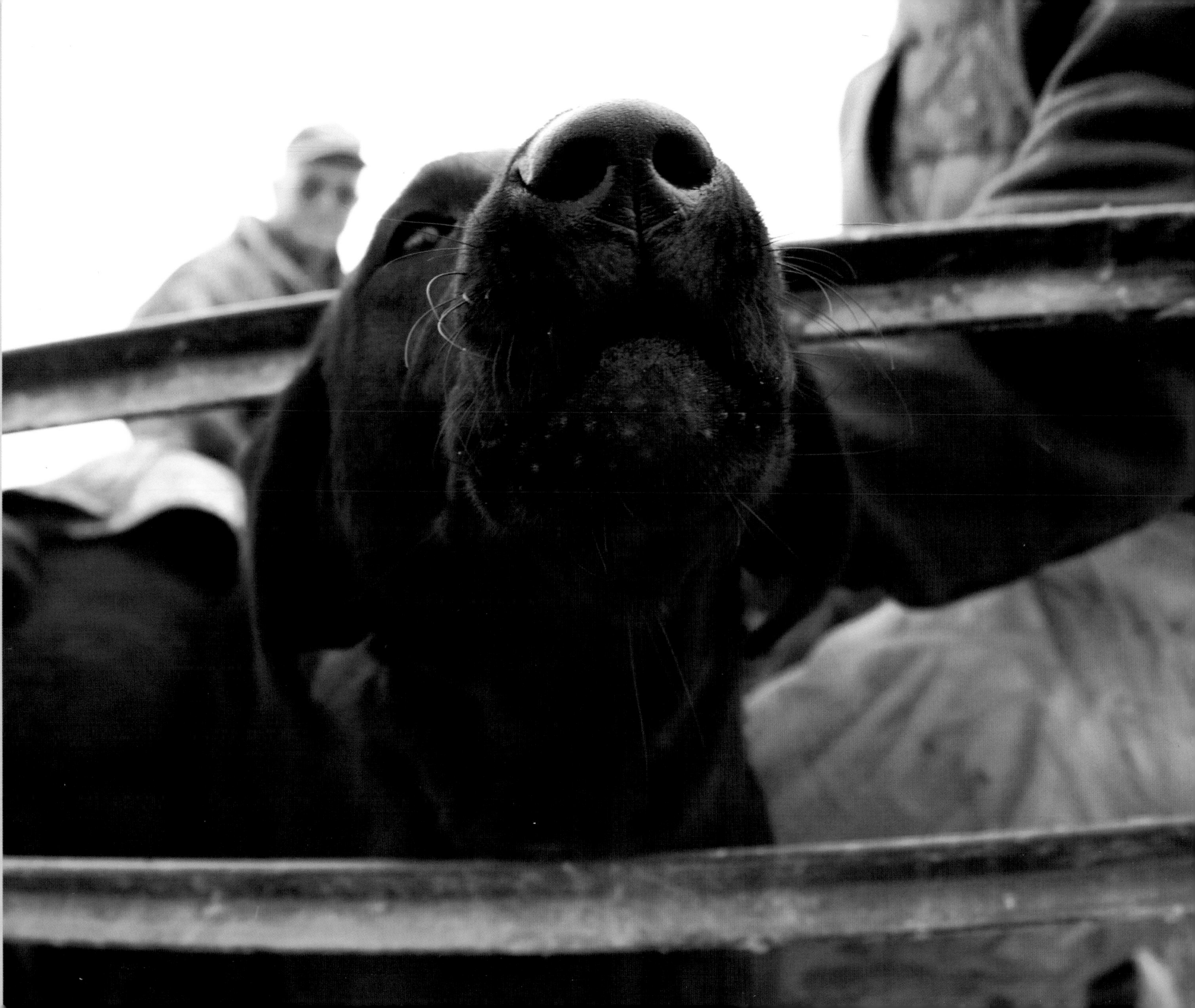

I am just a simple man to the rest of the world, but I am Superman in his eyes. He doesn't know that with him, I have confidence and pride, or that his loyalty and heart have taught me how completely flawed men really can be.

He's my partner regardless. That is a policy that he sets and one I live by.

He's my retriever.

© Larry Chandler

Hundred One

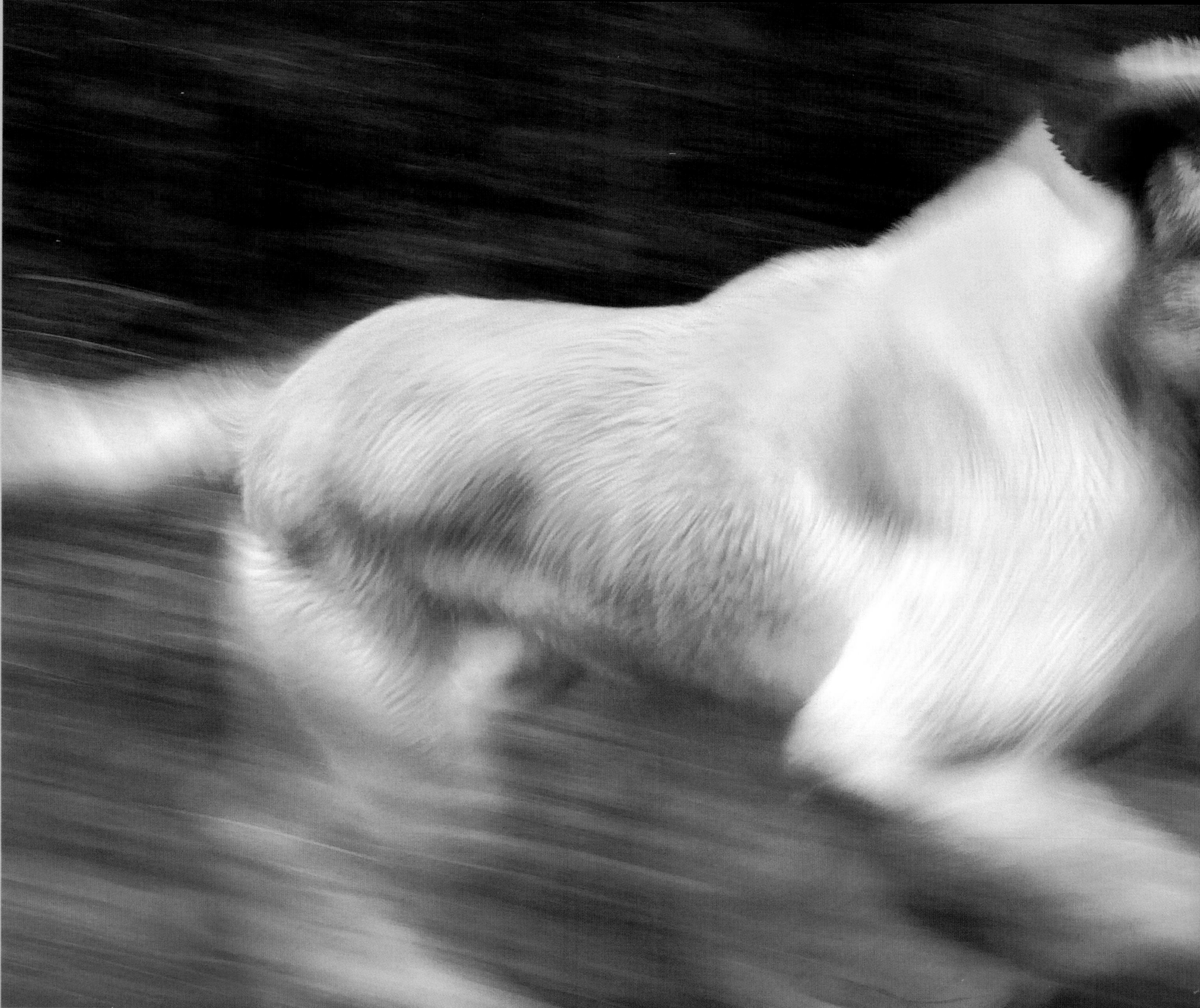

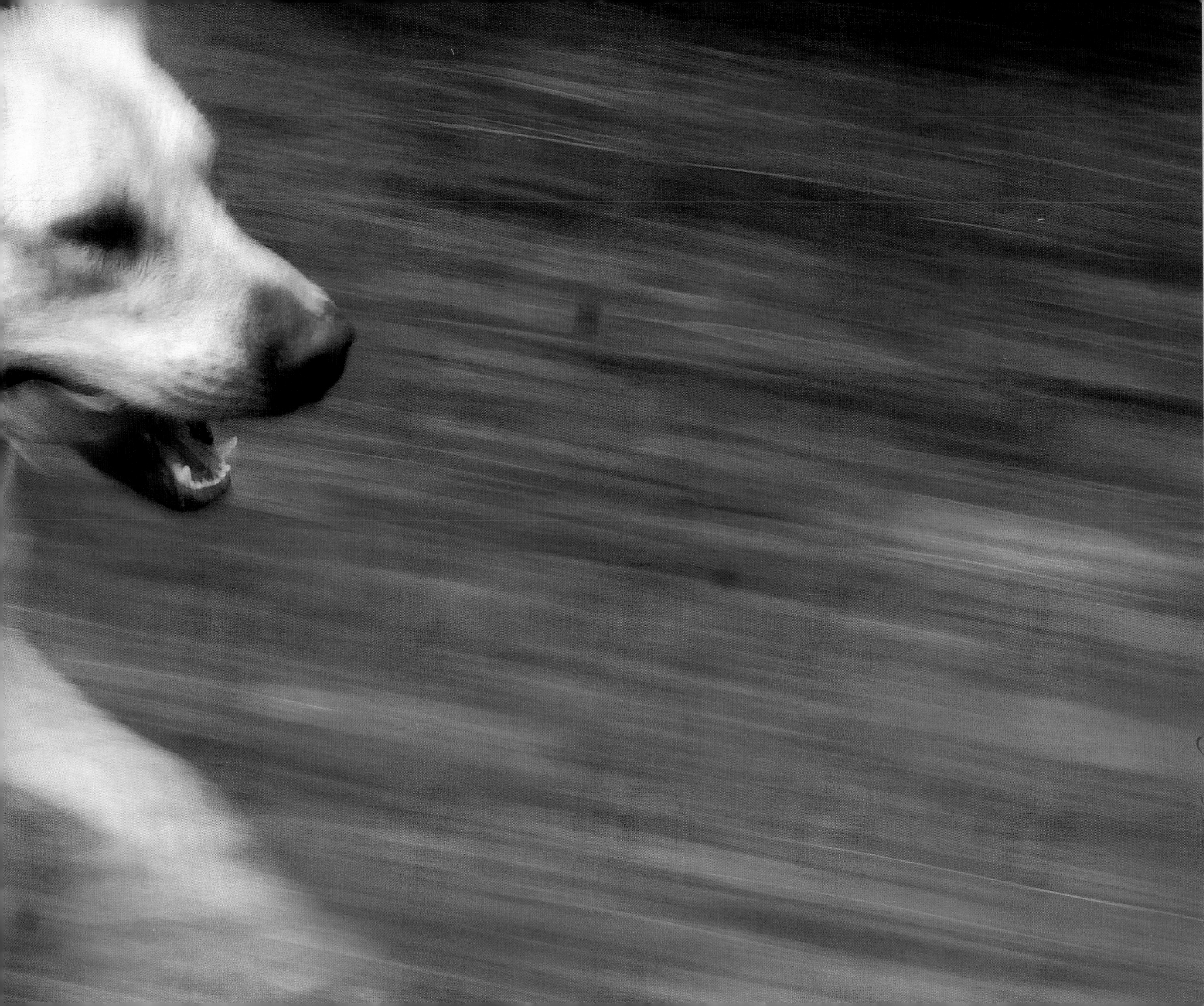

The more p
the more I

DOGS

"My dog training a
www.dog

CHAPTER SEVEN

The Watch

The memories are very clear of early duck hunts, when as a kid, you were constantly reminded to keep your head down.

"Keep that head down, boy! Or they'll see the whites of your eyes."

At a tender age, that was a very impressionable statement. It made you almost too scared to move. There was no way in the world I would be the one to flare a flock of ducks with the whites of my eyes. Those little slivers of white surrounding my irises stayed tucked away. I think I even learned to shoot a shotgun peeking out from behind the bill of my cap, the camouflage one with the white stitching around the John Deere logo.

Go figure!

As I grew older, I realized that whole whites-of-the-eyes thing was more paranoia than anything else. It was a simple way to keep some moon-pie-faced hunter from gazing at the wonders of ducks in flight and spooking them away.

Hundred Nine

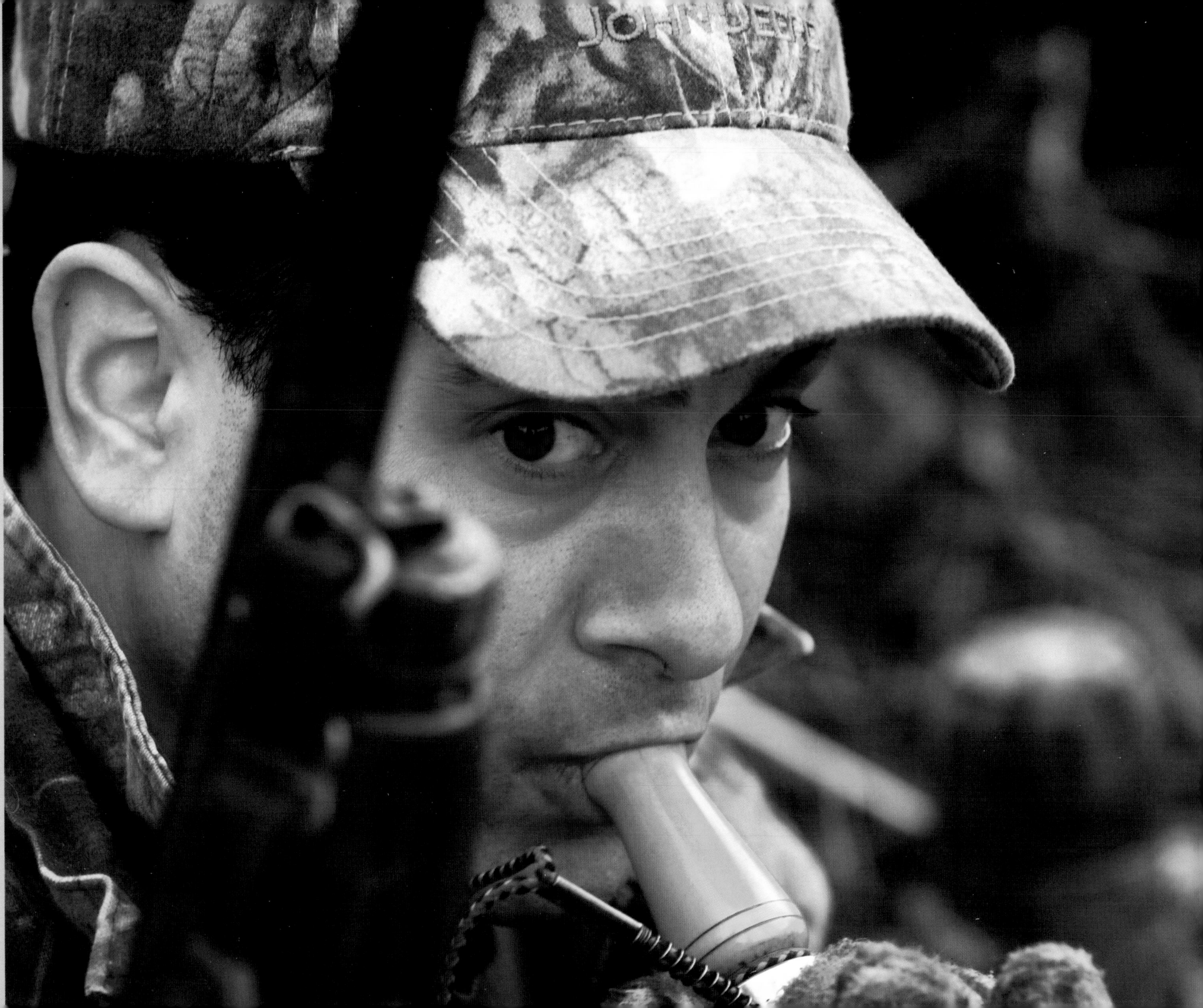

I even passed along that type of warning to young hunters unlucky enough to spend a day in the blind with me. Then I became wiser.

Becoming wiser is a gradual thing, something I'm still working on. I suspect it's something I'll be working on for a long time. At some point in this lifelong course, I learned better. I realized that a duck hunt was much more fun when viewed with open eyes pointed squarely to the sky. The scenery sure beat the backside of a cap's bill.

Now, I almost insist: "Look, watch, keep an eye on every detail, but don't move."

The reason: A duck hunt is 90 percent watching, mixed with all the other things like shooting, drinking coffee and telling stories. You can't appreciate the wonders of a duck hunt with your eyes focused on your feet or the back of a cap. The best storytellers relay their tales with an eye concentrating on what might be happening in the sky.

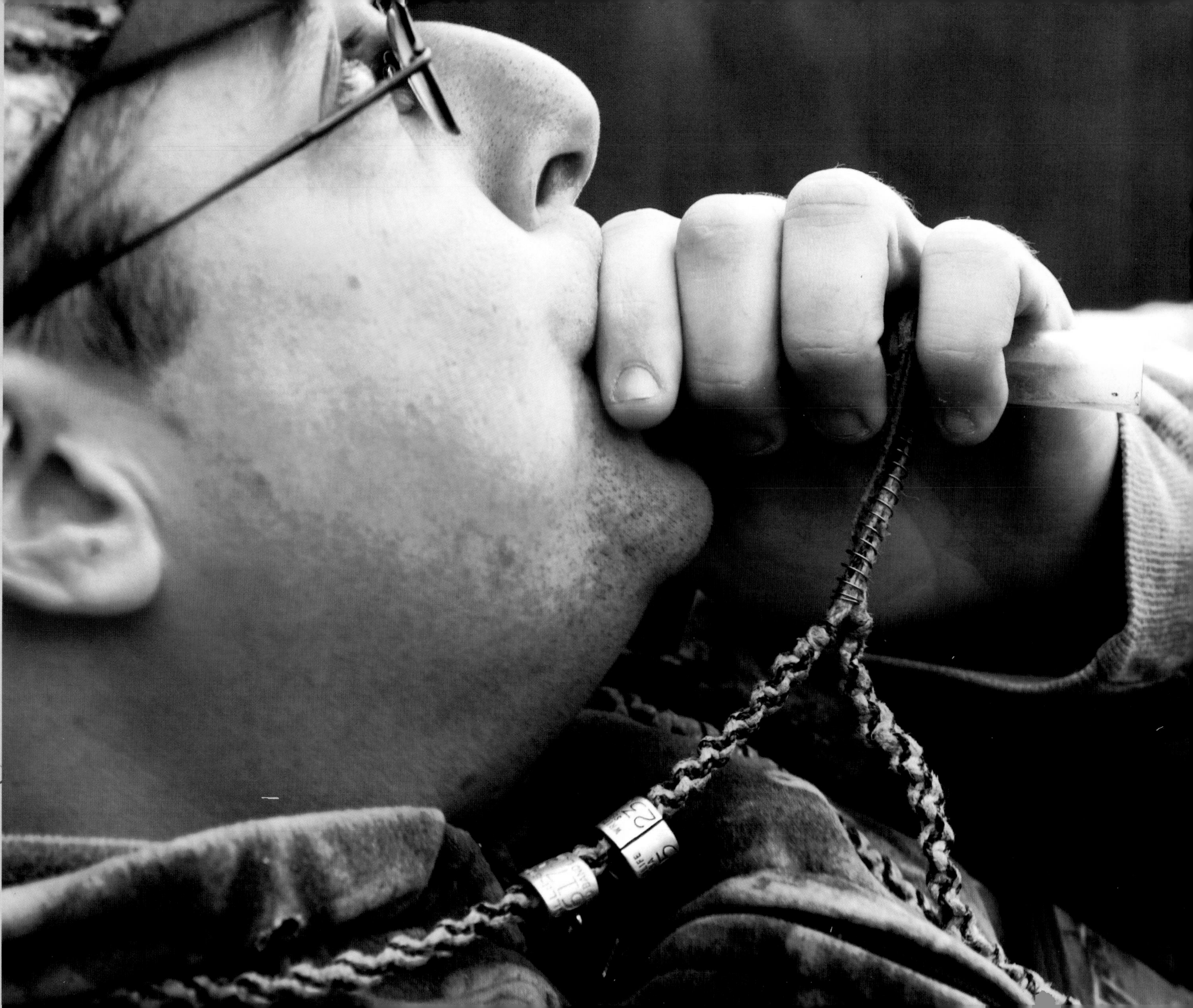

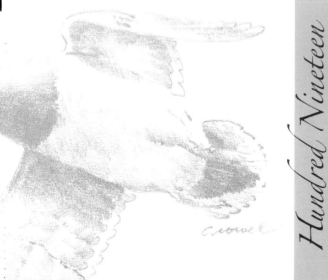

"The Watch" is what takes place for the biggest part of the day.

To understand the watch, you have to realize that eyes focused on a blank, blue sky are searching for specks appearing on the horizon that eventually form into flying ducks. Within those eyes is a silent pleading and hope that the next squadron of ducks will come close enough to work with a call and decoys.

They look for signs: a dip of a wing, the turn of a greenhead's neck, the setting of wings or the wavering and breaking up of a high flock, anything to indicate that maybe the game is about to be on.

It all starts with the whites of the eyes pointed up and out.

Hundred Nineteen

Th

CHAPTER EIGHT

Playground

You can tell at a young age whether a child will grow up to be a duck hunter. They will be the ones who head straight for the mud hole on a rainy day to stomp and kick and revel in the wetness.

There can be monkey bars, swings, maybe even a basketball court, but the real playground is that spot of water deep enough to splash around in.

When they grow older the playground just gets bigger.

The monkey bars are gone along with the swings, replaced with pin oaks sizable enough to play hide-and-seek with circling mallards. Mud holes are acres of rice fields and marsh, perfect for splashing about and in general getting justifiably covered with crud.

Duck hunt long enough and every wet spot big enough to float a decoy becomes a potential playground for a grown-up duck hunter. We're drawn to those places like an alcoholic to a pub.

We might not stop and play, but when we drive by a likely wet and muddy hole a duck might like, we can't help but look and rubberneck like it was a 12-car pile-up. That's because they all are a little bit different, each with their own set of redeeming values and beauty only a seasoned waterfowler understands.

Hundred Twenty Three

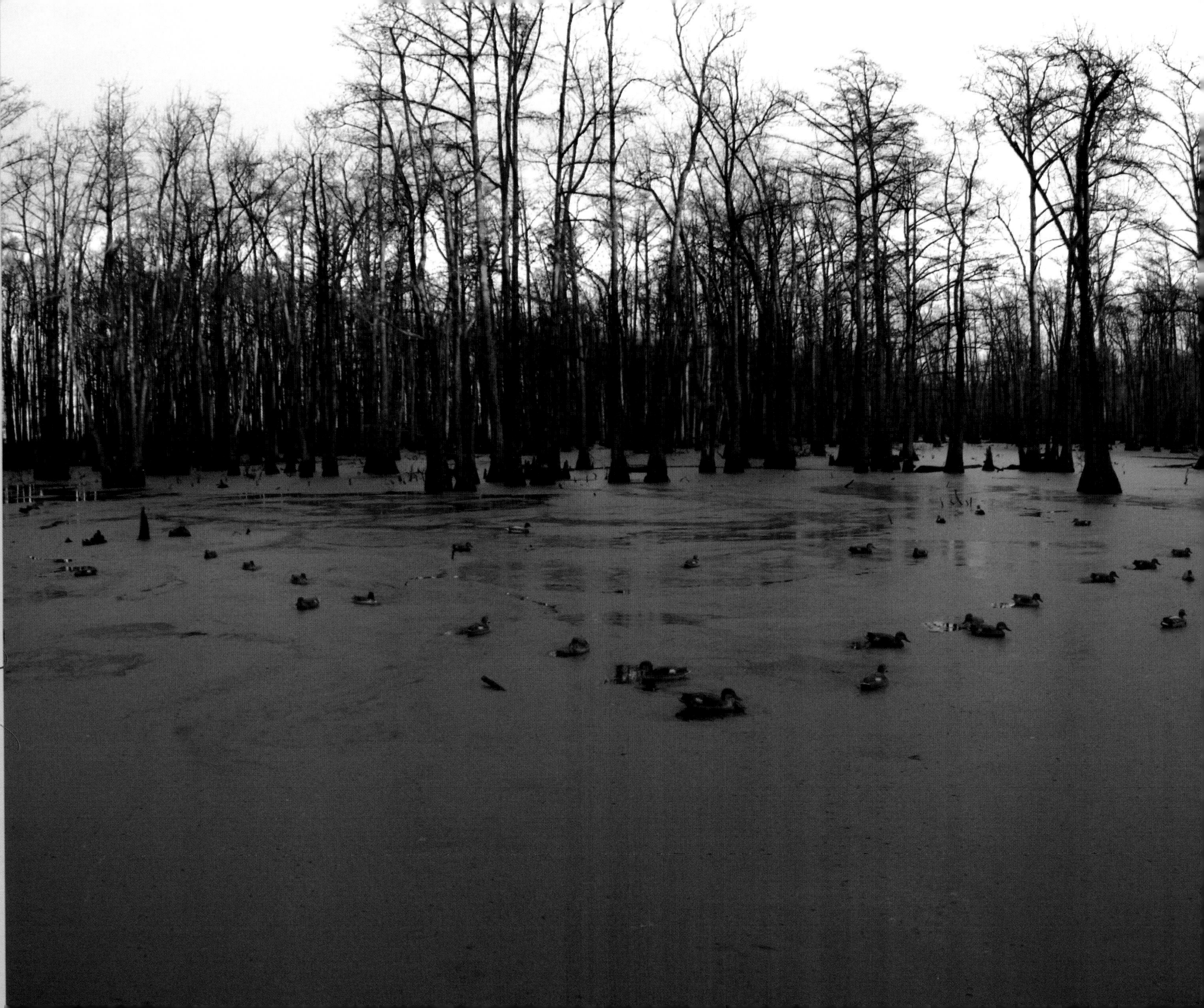

The duck hunter's playground includes oaks, buck brush, rice stubble, smartweed and mud mixed with copious amounts of water. They set the stage for the building of forts to gather in with other hunters. Some of the playgrounds are ideal to build bunkers and sink metal pits like foxholes.

All of them are places to hide to satisfy our conflicting phobias. On one hand we're agoraphobic, seeking to hide within the darkest hidey-holes of our playground. And on the other, we're claustrophobic, making sure that no matter where we hide it comes with a wonderful view of the entire playground, so we can see even the farthest speck in the sky in time to blow our calls and get ready for the moment those specks transform into cupping birds.

We are fiercely loyal to these playgrounds. Ducks Unlimited and Delta Waterfowl refer to these places as habitat. Try and take some of it away and the ire of people who love to roll around in the mud will befall you.

In the 1970's when the U.S. Army Corps of Engineers started draining and channelizing the Cache River in Arkansas, duck hunters all over the world, led by Rex Hancock, shut it down. Hancock referred to the effort as "an outrageous project and an insult to God's planning of the earth."

Two decades later Hancock's wisdom was recognized and credited when the Cache River received the designation of "Wetlands of International Importance."

That's just an illustration of how strongly a duck hunter feels about the muddy, wet places many folks want to get rid of. They are all places of importance, where we love to spend the day soaking in the sunrise and mud.

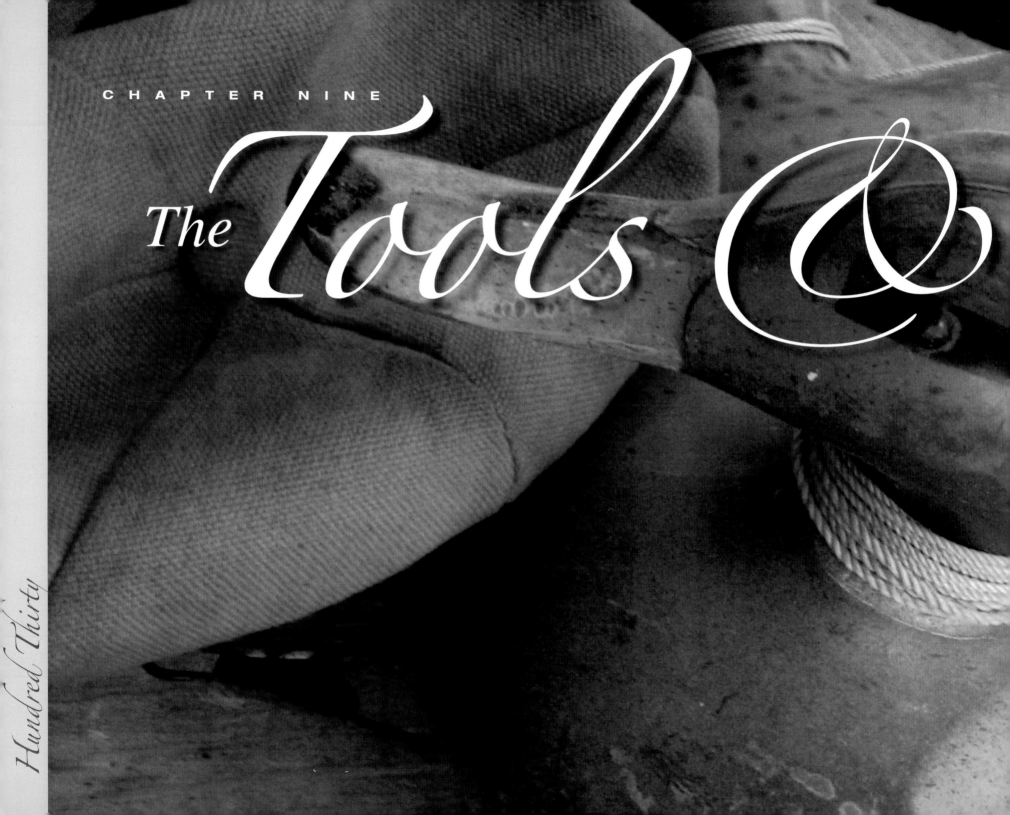

CHAPTER NINE

The Tools &

Toys

The uninitiated could make a good case that duck season is really all about the toys we play with.

No duck hunter is immune. Toys or tools, as they are referred to in the duck blind, are an integral part of duck hunting.

Don't believe it?

In Arkansas alone, estimates are that each day of duck season more than $8 million changes hands, much of that spent on buying the tools for a day's hunt like shotgun shells, boats, motors, ATVs, camouflage clothing, calls and decoys.

In Stuttgart, the accepted Duck Capital of the World, the largest retailer in town sells more than $2.1 million in shotgun shells each season.

Considering the average duck hunter can't have too many of those things, it would be hard to argue the point that these things are nothing more than toys. But why would you want to? One man's toy is another man's tool.

Chasing ducks in the mud and crud of the world often requires more than just a desire to play the game.

After all, how do you cross that creek or oxbow without a boat?

And if you feel the need to do it more comfortably, a little bit flashier and a whole lot faster than absolutely necessary, then so be it.

Of course, our grandfathers might have done it differently.

Hundred Thirty Three

Witness the trips of W.M. Apple, a former outdoor columnist for the *Arkansas Democrat*. He was a man in need of some toys in 1916 when he went hunting.

In those days, Apple's mode of travel was the Model T, and his duck hunt was not for the weak at heart. At that time, the road to Lonoke, the western edge of duck-rich east Arkansas, quit at the Pulaski County line.

"From there on you had no road except there was some semblance of a straight road from Lonoke to Hazen," Apple said. "We turned south at Hazen and we went across the prairie.

"There was nothing but trails across the prairie. We would leave Little Rock at 5 o'clock in the afternoon. We would drive all night and arrive at Bayou Meto Flat just in time to shoot ducks the next morning. It took about 12 hours to go 70 miles."

Bayou Meto Flat now is known as Bayou Meto Wildlife Management Area and today, even for an old-timer, the trip only takes a little more than an hour from Little Rock.

The Model T didn't allow for sleeping quarters. And hotel rooms or clubhouses had yet to come into existence.

So where did Apple camp?

"We didn't" Apple said. "After the rice had been shocked they would come along with a threshing machine. Then there would be a haystack — usually about 15 feet high and 50 feet in diameter. You would just bore a hole back in those things and crawl in.

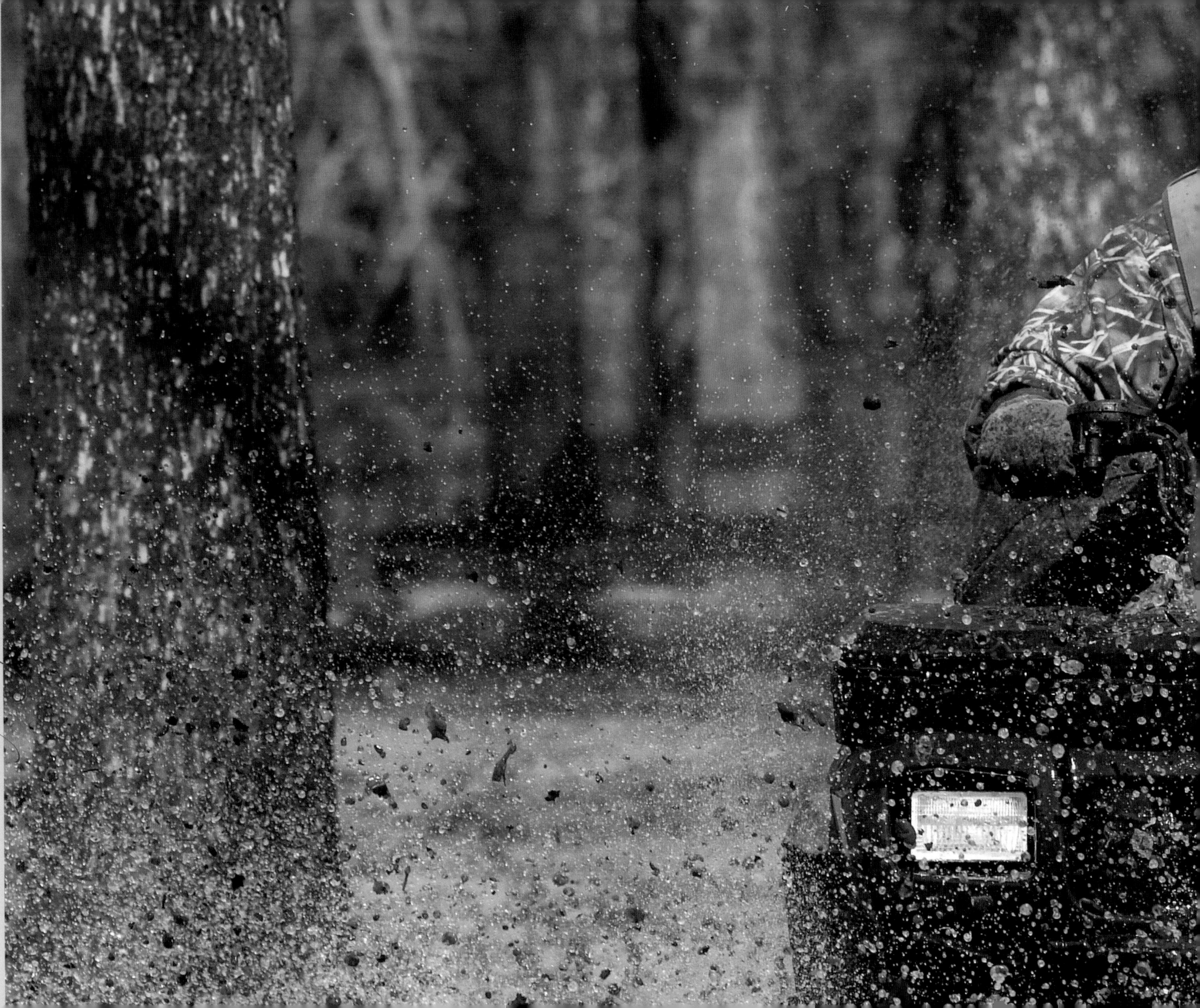

"They were the warmest things in the world to sleep in. The only trouble was crawling out into that predawn cold."

Sounds awesome, even romantic if there is such a word in a duck hunter's dictionary. Certainly it was hard-core, therefore necessary.

But don't lose a $1 bet to anyone that Apple wouldn't have done it an easier way if there was one. He'd trade that Model T for a Z71 in a heartbeat and the haystack for an RV if he had the choice.

That's the way life is these days: Every aspect of it revolves around a singular quest to make things easier.

Why would a duck hunter, despite his attention and respect for nostalgia, be any other way?

Tools, or toys, however you categorize them, are just part of duck season. It's a fact that will never change. That's because the driving force for the modern-day duck hunter and those of Apple's day are virtually the same.

They want to bag as many ducks for as many days as the law allows. And if that means utilizing things some folks might refer to as toys to get it done, then the price is well worth it.

And there are times when it's necessary.

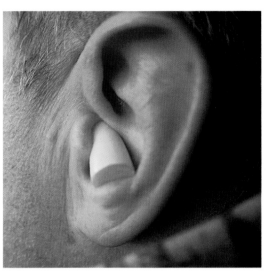

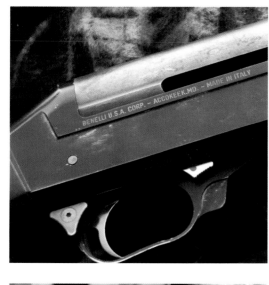

The idea of spending the night in the woods has its place when it comes to the lore of the sport until you're the one who has to do it. That's when a GPS becomes a tool.

Carrying a couple dozen decoys, a gun and several boxes of ammo while slogging through the mud in our cholesterol-laden society doesn't seem so proper when the turn of an ATV's key can add days to the season.

A necklace of duck calls with price tags that rivals the wife's jewels; a thermos that never cools; a heater that goes anywhere; neoprene boots that encase you up to your neck; decoys that move; camouflage jackets warm enough to withstand an arctic blast that hardly ever comes; dog stands that are more complicated than just sitting on a laydown or a beaver hut — these are just a few precious things that might be toys to some.

But in the relentless pursuit of ducks these are nothing more than tools of the trade.

WILL DUC

HUNT FOR FOOD

CHAPTER TEN

The Culture

The signs are everywhere.

A Ducks Unlimited sticker on a back glass; a Delta Waterfowl sticker on a bumper; a lanyard full of duck calls hanging from a rear-view mirror; or a duck head mounted on a trailer ball.

All these things indicate that this person is part of the brethren, a congregation of hunters. All of them are unabashedly proud to be a member of the group, and what a group it is.

There are no socioeconomic boundaries, no gender biases. The duck hunting culture is accepting of anyone who shares the passion. The signs are just a way of letting everyone know it exists.

- There is a radio station in Stuttgart, Ark., with the call sign KWAK;

- A bank in Jonesboro, Ark., with a bronzed mallard as big as a truck sitting in the lobby;

- A sporting goods store called Mack's Prairie Wings that is bigger than 90 percent of the churches in the country and is designed specifically for the duck hunter. It sits on the outskirts of a town that proclaims itself the "Duck Hunting Capital of the World."

There are ducks on ties and belts; sons that are named and christened "Drake." A coveted duck band, created to monitor duck migrations, is converted to a wedding band.

They are just small statements that duck hunting matters. It's more than just a hobby.

It's not only a way of life. It's a way to express ourselves and be recognized as more than just a fraternity of like-minded people.

This is a proud culture of gun-toting, camo-wearing folk unafraid to wear the signs.

Hundred Fifty

KWAK
AM 1240

2006 - 2007
Bayou Meto Morning by Scot Storm

Scot Storm was charged with creating the first stamp that would be an "In Your Face" mallard and flooded timber hunt. The stamp was the 26th in a program that has raised $10 million for conservation.

CHAPTER ELEVEN

The Stamps

The duck stamp measures only 1 7/16 by 2 1/8 inches but it might be the most important part of a duck hunter's season.

Without the Federal Duck Stamp, a hunter can't hunt anywhere. And in many states, like Arkansas, the State Duck Stamp is a passport to the legendary flooded pin oaks and rice fields.

2005 - 2006

Big Woods Mallards
by Larry Chandler

2004 - 2005

St. Francis River Mallards
by Ralph McDonald

2003 - 2004

Bayou LaGrue Mallards
by Zettie Jones

◄ *2002 - 2003*

Claypool's Reservoir by Phillip Crowe

Phillip Crowe's depiction of a stream of mallards twisting into Claypool's Reservoir includes the most ducks of any Arkansas Duck Stamp. Claypool's Reservoir is best known as the location of the only live television duck hunt ever aired. It took place in December 1956 on NBC. Its primary cast was more than 350,000 mallards.

2001 - 2002

Raft Creek Bottoms Canvasbacks
by Dave Maass

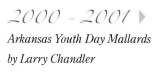

2000 - 2001 ▶

Arkansas Youth Day Mallards
by Larry Chandler

As its title suggests, this stamp celebrates the passing of passion to the next generation. Larry Chandler's image is an exact duplication of a hunt in northeast Arkansas where veteran Dick Gray introduced Marcus Huffer to flooded timber.

◀ 1999 - 2000

Seven Devils Wood Ducks
by Jim Hautman

Jim Hautman was on his way home from quail hunting in Texas when he stopped in Arkansas for a morning duck hunt. On that hunt he took thousands of photographs, all of which combined to capture what he felt were flooded timber's most brilliant colors.

1998 - 1999

Felsenthal Bottoms Mallards
by John Dearman

This is the first Arkansas Duck Stamp that included the hunter as a primary part of the overall scene. John Dearman captured it perfectly even though he had never been to Arkansas. His painting came from a series of photos taken by Larry Grisham.

1997 - 1998

Bayou DeView Green Timber Mallards
by Larry Chandler

Arkansas sells close to 100,000 stamps each season. The stamps have become more than just a passport to a legal hunt. In almost three decades the images portrayed on the Arkansas Duck Stamp have captured the essence of duck hunting like no photograph ever could.

All of them have a year attached, even though the scenes depicted are timeless. They've become collectibles adorning the walls of offices, dens and clubs. The money derived from the sale of those images goes directly toward conservation efforts to ensure that the scenes from these stamps are relived in perpetuity.

1996 - 1997

Arkansas County Mallards
by Phillip Crowe

This was the first duck stamp to feature the retriever. Phillip Crowe felt there was a "greater dimension to duck hunting" when a retriever was used. His painting proved the point. It quickly became one of the most popular stamps. It ushered in a standard where the retriever was featured in six of the next 11 stamps.

1995 - 1996

White River Mallards
by Larry Hayden

1994 - 1995 ▶

Honker at Lodge Corner
by Daniel Smith

Daniel Smith's Honker at Lodge Corner is dead-on accurate every fall. The sky, though, was inspired not by Arkansas' Grand Prairie, but from a skyline Smith observed a year earlier in Africa.

1993 - 1994

Grand Prairie Mallards
by Ken Carlson

1992 - 1993

Shirey Bay Shovelers
by Jim Hautman

Hundred Fifty Seven

1991 - 1992

Sulphur River Wigeons
by Daniel Smith

1990 - 1991 ▶

Point Remove Black Duck and Mallards
by Dave Maass

Dave Maass' print comes from an Arkansas flooded timber hunt, where a Black Duck led a flock of mallards through the woods and right into the lap of Maass. The sight mesmerized the artist so much he failed to raise his gun. His rendition of the moment became one of the most popular stamps of all time.

A book dedicated to the images of a duck season would not be complete without the inclusion of those on the stamp. They speak to a duck hunter in different ways, because they, like no other image, extend the memory of every season to last a lifetime. This is the collection of the 26 years of Arkansas Duck Stamps.

◀ *1989 - 1990*

Wingmead Mallards
By Phillip Crowe

Wingmead is best known as Edgar M. Queeny's estate, where the video and book "Prairie Wings" was created in the 1940s. When the estate was sold in 1976, Elvis Presley was rumored to have bid on it.

1988 - 1989

Cache River Pintails
by Maynard Reece

The plight of the pintail is a well-known story among duck hunters. But that wasn't the case in the 1980s, when Maynard Reece painted this stamp to help bring attention to the pintail.

1987 - 1988

Hurricane Lake Wood Ducks
by Robert Bateman

1986 - 1987

Black Swamp Mallards
by Jack Cowan

1985 - 1986

Bayou DeView Mallards
by Ken Carlson

1984 - 1985

Bois D'Arc Pintails
by Larry Hayden

◄ *1983 - 1984*
Black River Green-Winged Teal
by Dave Maass

Dave Maass' Black River Teal was a re-sult of Maass' first duck hunting to trip to Arkansas. He was there as a judge for the World Duck Calling Championship and was inspired by the trip. Recognized as the nation's premier waterfowl artist, Maass has never missed an Arkansas duck season since.

▲
1982 - 1983
Big Lake Wood Ducks
by Maynard Reece

◄ *1981 - 1982*
Bayou Meto Mallards
by Lee LeBlanc

Lee LeBlanc began his career in Hollywood as an animator for Looney Tunes and Merrie Melodies. His rendi-tion of mallards in Bayou Meto kicked off the Arkansas Duck Stamp program, the most successful state duck stamp and print program in the country.